CW00518759

WAKING AT FIVE HAP

WAKING AT FIVE HAPPENS AGAIN

Poems

Alison Prince

Mariscat Press / HappenStance

© Alison Prince 2016

ISBN 978 0 946588 83 1

Designed and typeset by Gerry Cambridge
www.gerrycambridge.com

Printed by Glasgow Print & Design Centre
197 Bath Street, Glasgow G2 4HU
www.GlasgowPDC.co.uk

Published by

Mariscat Press
10 Bell Place, Edinburgh EH3 5HT
hamish.whyte@btinternet.com
www.mariscatpress.com

and

HappenStance
21 Hatton Green, Glenrothes,
Fife KY7 4SD
nell@happenstancepress.com
www.happenstancepress.com

Contents

Thank you to Nell and Hamish, without whom
this book would not exist

Reckoning

There is no column in which to enter
sudden rainbows and the purred credit
of a cat that used to run away.
No auditor will ever scrutinise
the totals, no unhappy creditor
is going to get paid for moments seen
as marked in red ballpoint on debit page.
It doesn't work that way. This reckoning
weights the years of non-accountancy
and absence of all tangible profit
against a small blue marble, trowel-turned
from the cold earth of spring, and finds
a perfect balance.

Cabbage Whites

Two Cabbage Whites are having sex
on heart-shaped leaves of columbine
in the dry bed. Such fluttering,
such urgency, they do not see
a third one just a bramble-arm away.
He darts in when they part, but up they sail
over the white mock-orange, held by love
like silk circling a bobbin made of air,
winding, winding, an exclusive dance
in which each new move comes
with the beauty of a thing long known,
this first and only time.

The Form

Is there water within 30 metres of your house?

The burn swallows the lawn sometimes.
It's running brown today because the rain
has washed a bank away
somewhere up there in the forestry.
At calmer times
the heron comes and stands in it
as though in a stone pool at Versailles.

Is your house within 50 metres of the sea?

On the high tide and a south-east wind
waves burst over the sea wall last week,
drowning a lorry piled with Sitka spruce.
You need not know that I drove through
a sky as full of water as a fairground ride,
chugging the engine so the exhaust pipe
would blow hot gas out in a hoped defence
against the rush of brine and bladderwrack.
The brakes still squeal but Angus says
they will dry out if frequently hard-used.

Are there trees within 10 metres of your house?

The vast laburnum, you will be glad to hear,
blew down when its load of yellow blooms
overwhelmed it in a summer storm.
You need not know the bird cherry still stands.
Its branches help to keep the phone line safe
in winter gales.

Failure to answer any of these questions
may invalidate your application.

Had I not re-hocked the house
I'd bin your form and all pretences
of security. Risk did me well
when I owned nothing, and will do well again
when nothing reclaims me; when I have gone
into the wind and the laburnum wood
and the outrageous power of the sea.

Missing the Boat

After that long drive, it's too late.
No cars queue up at the loading ramp,
all the successful ones have gone.
Stern lights recede across the sea
under a round, indifferent moon.

Got side-tracked, didn't you.
Stopped for coffee and the view
and the production of a child or two.
So the boat has gone.
But once its wash stops sliding thin reminders
through the marram grass, new joy comes in.

Sit on a rock and stretch the toes
in sea-water so cold, it shocks again
as it did only yesterday
when your soft-padded feet
were still growing.

Interlude

My father was playing Chopin.
Clear evening light
shone through the poplar trees
where every leaf was still.
The night raid would begin
but not just yet. I could sit on the garden wall
a little longer, the bunks underground
could wait. Clear notes,
secure in their patterning, floated
and without hurry arrived at their end.
And then, perfectly timed,
the siren went.

Sideways

The sideways seat behind the driver
faces the luggage rack.
A golf bag slithers on the top
of stacked-up cases and beyond
the world slides right to left,
proving that this is not America
or some other foreign part. It's known—
the Dyemill bend where squirrels run,
the bridge over the burn, the yellow broom,
silage piled behind Jim's slow tractor,
the hill's outline.

It all moves on but gets stuck in the mind.
With eyes closed, the things seen are sharp again,
each wheelie bin, each clump of daffodils,
and yet they are changing.
Primroses fade, bus engines require overhaul.
A man gets in who last year said goodbye
to his gapped teeth and has a straight, white smile,
and at the mustard factory
a woman clambers painfully aboard
who didn't need two sticks until this spring.

Facing forward calms the rush of passing,
makes you feel more part of it—but all
the forward-looking seats were occupied.
Side-on, there's no defence against seeing.

Crumbs

The robin knows that when the car returns
and stops under the leafless cherry tree
a god gets out and may with luck notice
the bird with feathers lifting in the wind.
This god may bring bread from its house
if so inclined. But if a ring-ring sounds
it will attend to that instead, or it may be
too busy carrying its new things in.
Faith, the robin understands,
is a matter of coincidence.

Glass

Not quite dawn.
Bats are whirling close outside the window
that's a crack open. Dark faces
glance in, then are gone.
Science fiction twitches at the mind.
Combat battalions?
No. Bats are like us,
they bear live babies that they feed.
It's just they have black fur
and wings and hooky thumbs.
Light grows. Their zooming thins.
A single one skims past
for a last look in.

Wake again. Bright sun.
Up, reach for toothbrush, turn tap on—
the plughole has grown little black elbows
that creep and struggle, wet.
So this is what they wanted in the night.
Gather him up. Or her. Go out.
Under the alpine strawberries
it will be cool at least, kept from the sun.

Ten minutes afterwards, he's gone. Or she.
Not rescued, for this is bat-sleeping time.
If the little batteries run out
a bat mother will sky-comb all alone,
the wrong side of the glass.

Sannox Bend

A man stands in the road
before the Sannox bend, hand raised.
'I've twenty yowes coming.'
Hear them first, the pattering,
then see the mass of them,
horned heads held high, wary,
a boy behind them and a dog
lapping its loops,
keeping its fleeced flotsam intact.
Gated, they turn as one
to stare back at the road
like fish facing upstream,
gaze gradually round
and start grazing again.
Drive on up the new-dunged river bed.

Being Them

I know a lot about Them.
Who wanted to breed butterflies,
who got caught driving
after eight pints of heavy.
Whose wife left him for a man
who said he cleaned windows
but in reality nicked whatever
he could lay hands on.

I don't easily put face to name
and so there are moments of thinking,
Ah, this is you. Or, *You're the one*
they told me to be careful of.

The odd thing is,
when eyes have met
they're either friends or will get thrown
back into the wide sea of Themness.
Not every thing you catch
is useful or desirable.

Let's not get sidetracked
into this metaphor of fishing.
The real skill is to swim.
Or, at least, to stay afloat.

Burial

Donald Muldoon, the undertaker,
has himself been taken.
He lies under a rectangle
of granite chips, with a headstone
designed by his own hand.
His horses predeceased him
when a motor hearse replaced
the plumes and dung
of road-walked funerals.

At his burial on the hillside
there was mourning
for more than Donald's death.
A girl came, riding a black pony.
None of us knew who she was.
The little horse stood quietly,
front hooves together in respect,
and bowed its head.

Wartime

They would have been old ladies now
except the Luftwaffe arrived
earlier than usual that night.
The flat above the chemist's shop
and its tiled roof were no protection
so when the anti-aircraft guns
opened up, they ran across the road
towards the public shelter.

A bomb killed one of them
but the other stumbled on.
Only inside the curtain
did the dim light show her hands
holding the spilled wreckage
of her abdomen.
She died before they could find anyone
who might have helped.

Her parents asked my mother
whether she thought I'd mind
if the baby doll that had been mine
went in her grave. I'd called her Betty.
She had blue eyes that opened
when you picked her up.
But in the wartime shortages
you passed things on.

Biggin Hill

In nineteen-thirty-nine, we watched
three Spitfires taking off from Biggin Hill.
They raced towards us, chevron
formation, two rising, the centre one
down a bit. We ducked.
It brushed the hedge.
Leaf-spattered, deafened,
scared and thrilled, we watched
the upward roar into the sky
where, a year later, deadly sport
would rivet us. We stared up,
tin-hatted by then, hands shadowing
our eyes, saw smoke-burst start,
cheered at a spinning fall, or groaned.
Felt the earth shake.

Teaching in the school
at Biggin Hill a decade on,
kids shrieked, 'Miss, Miss, he's got a gun!'
Jimmy from the camp MQ, aged six,
hefted a revolver in both hands.
Tough kid. From Singapore,
Aden, Beirut, many postings, many dads
who came and stayed the night.
He never spoke, just barked
under his desk. One day he tripped
and hit his head. And cried.
I took him on my lap and still he cried,
went soft in my arms with his weeping.
I told the other fifty-nine of them,
'Jimmy's a bit upset. Just get on quietly.'
They nodded and did that.
Such things, in Biggin Hill, were understood.

Resistance

White fog blocked out the Alps.
In the small café
the owners' grandmother
peeled potatoes behind the counter.
Young men made jokes in German
about the peasantry.

Job complete, the old lady
made for the door
with her full bowl of water
and potato peelings.
Someone opened it for her—
but the bowl had somehow tipped
into the lap of the chief mocker.
'Je m'excuse,' she said
without a smile.

The Swiss laughed so much
that small black choughs flew up, clacking,
into their vast, white mountains.

Vienna, 1952

You needed a grey card then
to get into Vienna, but a man
driving an open truck let me
hide under sacks.
'If they find you at the checkpoint,
I don't know you're there, *verstehen?*'
'*Ja. Danke schön.*'

Exchanges of *Grüss Gott*
at the checkpoint.
Keep very still.

At St Stephans Kirche, there he is,
waiting on the steps as we agreed
ten days ago in Italy.
He took me through the rubble
of the Ringstrasse
to a solitary standing block.

In a top room
his mother served stewed raspberries.
So sweet, she and the fruit.
The window looked over a wasteland
where a Ferris wheel did not yet turn.

Reeds

In among the tall reed palisades
beside the duckpond in the park
were spaces where the two of us could hide.

The sun went down but we did not go home,
telling each other that we were
constantly scolded. Some worry
might improve their attitude.

Our mothers were calling us.
We stayed silent, wanting them to learn
what it would be like when they were known
as mothers whose children had gone away
to live like ducks or tadpoles in the pond.

It fell quiet. Then they came again,
this time with our fathers, who poked sticks
through the reeds and found us.
They were extremely cross.
Our eyes met, unsurprised.
You see? They weren't glad
to have us back at all.

I didn't know for many years
what nightmare must have underlain
their screams of love.

Riches

The man who mended my computer
wanted no money but was glad
to fill a plastic bag with raspberries.
A tenor given lifts to choir practice
gave me six brown eggs
with a soft feather in the box.
A neighbour brought honey from his bees
when I was ill, and somebody
left a pot of soup on the doorstep.

I gave a felled laburnum tree
to a wood turner met in the Post Office.
He gave me a full-ripe pear
turned from laburnum wood,
rich and heavy in the empty hand.

The Watcher

'You have to have some teeth out this morning.'

> He thinks about it with his usual calm.
> 'How many teeth?'

His mother isn't sure.
'Just the bad ones.
It's in the hospital so you'll get gas.
You're just a child. You'll go to sleep
and when you wake up it'll all be done.'

> He frowns.
> 'Don't want to sleep. I have to watch.'

'You can't watch yourself, you daft cuckoo.'

> 'I can. I do it all the time.'
> He sees he must explain.
> 'When I have my teeth pulled out
> I want to see them doing it.
> So I must be there.'

She wonders again whether her son
is quite right in the head.

> The watcher stares at broken holes
> in the boy's teeth and feels them with his tongue,
> grieving for him about what must be done.
> A big mistake. Tears come.
> *Look, look, the boy is crying.*
> And the watcher weeps as well.

'Sweetheart, don't cry,' his mother says. 'You're not alone.'

He could have told her that.
But it would have been a lie.
He is alone and so am I
since I am him.
We are not two but one.

The Shed

'Mum. There's a man in the shed.'
'A man? Are you sure?'
She dries her hands.
'Let's go and see.'

Inside the shed, nothing except
the lawnmower and garden tools.
Last year's bamboos lean in a tea chest,
their cobwebs quite still.

The child points her hand.
'Look. You can see him.'
Her mothers swallows hard.
'How big is he?'

In the hospital they'd said
her daughter was unusual.
'Huge. He's bending down so he fits in.'
'Is he a nice man, do you think?'

'Oh yes. He gave me a mouse.'
She brings out a half-closed hand.
Long tail on one side. On the other,
whiskers quivering.

Gazing at the dusty roof
her face is radiant. 'You see,
you see? He shines.'
Her mother shuts her eyes.

Her daughter has told her she is blind.
Looking is useless. But the radiance
breaks through her closed lids, as red
and bright as new-spilled blood.

Surgeon

'Your lungs are in a shocking state,' he said.
I wondered whether to apologise, but he
was still note-riffling, much dissatisfied
at finding nothing that could be excised
and take the blame.

I backed the car out from its parking space
between pine trees above the sea
and the old magic worked again.
I was happy. But how can magic be
prescribed and costed as a therapy?

Toast

He moves the table with me on it
like a piece of toast under the grill.
Retreats behind his screen
until the bleep.
Afterwards, still in a cotton gown
with untied tie-ups down the back,
I ask what he's looking for.
'Cancer of the bone.
But I can see no sign of it.'

Alternative suspect dismissed.
Box ticked.

What stays in place
is the narrowing of silted lungs
the double-time thumping
of wonky heart. They will not operate
until all the boxes have been ticked.
Can't blame them, but time ebbs.
Fiddle about, eliminate.
Not nice, at the funeral,
to know they were too late.

Mr Thrower

He was a carpenter.
Got splinters in his neck one day
from carrying timber on his shoulder.
My mother took them out with a needle
and Dettol.

In the summer of the flying bombs
he looked out of the shelter
as an engine cut,
assuming it would glide.
They mostly did
but this dropped like a stone.

His body lay where it had fallen,
just inside the shelter.
His head, outside and separate,
stared skyward
at what was to come.

Raspberries

I have not picked raspberries like this
for half a century. At that lost time
Uncle Harry kept them orderly,
tied in at shoulder height.
These reach above my head,
unbegrudged for the blackbirds to take
since such a cornucopia
overflows the bowl and polybag.

Their firmness lifts away from a white core
easily. Clinging means you must come back
later, when a carmine adolescence
has matured to full, ruby-rich red.
Cueillez les fleurs de ta jeunesse
and of your age. There is no certainty
that you will see such amplitude again.

Dangerous Men

I can only love dangerous men.
The others can be excellent
members of committees, pianists
and keepers of Labradors, but where
is the prickle of an unknown risk,
the sense of muscle underneath the skin,
the possibility of sudden hurt?
They are the unpredictable, my kind,
who can break a neck with quick hand's edge,
who have themselves grown up in cruelty
and watch with eyes yellow as tiger-glance
for weakness. When threatened with boredom
they retreat on silent, long-clawed paws
into the heaving jungle of the mind,
and that is where I want to follow them.

The Break

The dream begins again.
The curve of street,
the open bomb-site, are familiar.
I know this place.
But I do not.

Wake up.

The dream begins again
or else the ghost of it
lays fingers on the neck.
I am a rabbit now,
before the break.

Kids

It was as if the children who were killed
were always the good, the virtuous
who did their homework properly and never played
in bomb craters and taped-off sites.
We were not gamblers—no winnings to count
and no applause. Quite the reverse, in fact.
'Where have you been?'

Hurling a Spitfire through the sky, mother.
Manning an ack-ack gun.
We were not old enough, but we invented it.
We practised bandaging,
wanted to drive an ambulance
or fire engine with clanging bell.

Tin hats were all too real,
the odd balance of heaviness
and canvas strap.
People in uniform banished our dream.
They had no time for us.
We were just kids,
though not what you could call children.

Benevolence

Take nothing for granted,
my father said, a canny lad
born north of Leeds.
His life was ruled by morning train
at eight fourteen and coming home
on the six ten. He had his tea
and sat for a bit reading Goethe
or Tolstoy, then got up
and went to the piano.
Schubert, Chopin, Beethoven.
He never complained.
If you can climb stairs, he said,
without needing your hands on them,
that's benevolence enough
for any man.

Islands

Missing the sea, cast up like bladderwrack
beyond all tides to dry black in a sun
blocked off by square, high building tops, I am
aching with desperation to be back
on the island where each casual gaze
is outward to the linking, steady line
of the horizon. Yet struggling to find
ease shows that the eye has subtle ways
of reassurance. Buddleia has grown
fat purple blossoms halfway up a wall
and further on a dandelion unrolls
its gold in a crack between paving stones.
Here is a tree that the Council has put
in a littered gap. See how it tries
to prosper. Chopped by its leaves, the sky
is the same sky that will glow at sunset
over the far-off sea. This time will pass.
Meanwhile, these little skerries of relief
offer a hopscotch of non-urban life,
rock after rock. Privet, a patch of grass,
a gutter puddle left from last night's rain.
Such things do not perceive human distress
or know themselves as lovely, effortless
islands of safety for a marooned brain.

Reprieve

Be careful.
Just because death came
close enough to feel its non-breathing
and then stepped back,
you are no matador.
The blackness does not charge
in some bullring
but waits in yoghurt pot and coffee cup,
tapping the fingernails.
The reprieve papers are not signed.
Stand at the cliff's edge.
Watch great birds
rest their easy weight on the north wind.

Letty, by Glenashdale Burn

My little granddaughter is staring
at a heron that maintains its place
with grey wings folded for the last time,
head bent back, bill raised to wait
for what is going to come out of the sky.

She takes a step towards it, and it gives
a raucous screech of warning, half-strangled
in its dying throat. She flinches and cries.
I pick her up and try to explain
that the bird is busy dealing with
a change in everything.

We look back for a moment. The heron
hasn't moved, although its eyes are closed.
'It doesn't mind, does it?' she says. And we walk on,
her warm weight on my hip a fresh blessing.

Dread

It starts with disbelief, as when a child
is told she's having teeth out this morning.
I can't. I won't. I don't have to.
Run off and climb the apple tree
protected by deep mud.
She'll get her head round it, just give her time.

An operation on the heart next month.
Mostly it works, they say.
In with a chance.
Meanwhile the garden is the safest place.
Above tall trees, cloud-shadows
constantly just fail to kill the sun.

November Week

Monday

In the strange land of kitchen table
and sleepless bed,
thick blue veins still run
on narrowed hands become mysterious,
an interlocked conundrum
the brain can't understand.

The table's patterning of figured oak
was laid down in its early saplinghood.
These fingernails will grow
after the hour of death and then mingle
with earth's lovely chemistry.
Comprehension is superfluous.
Trust is enough.

Tuesday

Silent as yet, the coming storm
is in the wave caps vanishing
at the horizon.

Bare trees move
only a fraction.
No gulls fly.

The wind, south-westerly,
is speeding up.
A car passes.

Its headlights die behind the hill.
The cat is warm, curled on my lap.
We are alive.

Wednesday

Hello? Is anybody there?
It's over three months now since your consultant
said in a video conference he'd schedule me
for heart valve surgery within
four or five weeks. I know you are busy
but if it meant anything—
which it may not have done—
I need one of your buff envelopes
that state an appointment.

There is this surge of hope, you see,
each time post comes, but it's always
Greenpeace or a donkey sanctuary
or Books for Africa or Médécins
Sans Frontières, whom I support.
It's just, sometimes I wish there was
an envelope supporting me.

Thursday

Stepping stones are not reliable.
They turn beneath the feet
and the river runs fast.
No overhanging branch worth clutching at.
Rely on balance.
Hold the hands wide, as though sensing
a trembling pole, and take a step.
Transfer the weight. Now a next one.
Ignore the voices from the bank
insisting on protocol. Too late for that.
Keep moving on. Watchers may hope
for sudden comedy, the slip,
the splash, the floundering,
the phoning for an ambulance.
It may not be like that.
Go on, go on. Stone after stone.

Friday

This forest has no trees.
These vertical risings
are question marks.

Their sickle shapes
slice up the sky
in new-moon curves.

No trees. No carving
of hearts, no crying out
of the message,

I was here once.
No bark. No sap
under the fingernails.

Saturday

It might be easier to cast off lethargy
if it could be explained, or failing that,
discussed. Does the persistent anaemia
come from an unknown incidence
as surgeons assume? Or is it,
as lesser medics tend to theorise,
caused by a failed aortic valve, correctable
by risky operation? Take your pick.
Either way, the tiredness spreads
like creeping shadow, too intense
to shift. The time factor acts as
a fast corrosion, eating down the chance
of survival at a rate, they estimate,
of ten per cent per annum. So right now
it's eighty per cent possible that I
won't die on the table. That gets less
with each month gone. I write a letter sometimes
to the NHS, not cross but just reminding them
I'm running out of time.
There's going to come a crisis point
when no-one thinks the chance sustainable.
In the vernacular, this might be put
concisely in four words, *Fuck off and die.*
And that's OK, eventually. Meanwhile,
it would be nice to have a word with somebody.
Hello? Is anybody there? Listen
to the silence.

Sunday

It was a hard weekend.
The talking. The conviviality.
The need to fend off the feeling
that it was all too much.
The desperate desire to be in bed.

While still afloat, one must keep paddling
to keep a little way ahead.
The frightful fiend is close behind,
not treading but drifting
with an absent smile.
Don't turn the head and look,
or in a flash it's at the table,
in the coffee cups, the washing-up,
a dread darker than tea-stain,
an uninvited guest
who will not eat or smile.

Time is shortening.
Whether to squander or prioritise
is a hard choice, since the criteria
are not objective.
Its rules, though, are stern.
Look at the straight line of the horizon.
Look at the hill.
Look at the veins in your own wrist.
Look at the spider rescued from the bath.
Be in a state of worship as existing
becomes increasingly miraculous.
While the imagined span dwindles
its value concentrates, just as the earth
presses itself into diamonds.

Antidote to Boredom

The grey cat savages the kitchen mat,
chewing at its throat while her hind claws
slash and disembowel it.

She was probably bored.
That's why cat conferences
are loud and short and usually end
with rushing over roof tops
and screaming. No cat would ever sit
through PowerPoint without
regurgitating something on the floor.

Fixing the Memory

He snowcemmed the house last year, dead white,
cleaned the place up. Scraped off
the mud-built martins' nests
from below high eaves.
The birds came back and fretted
because it smelled all wrong.

Migrants can bring
nothing except a knowing of the place
where they were born—but the pattern
was torn like a shot wing. They had to build
on a wall east-facing, where the sun
could not warm nestlings that must be
fed constantly until the time to fly.

Winter stripped the newness of the paint
and killed the smell, so joyful twitterings
filled the sky at the next May return.
New nests were built on the lost line
of old ones, two broods hatched and then a third,
fed partly by the earlier egg-young
who, unknowing, fixed the memory
in more minds, more wings
to carry it across more foreign seas.

The Beautiful Game

A man is playing football on the beach
all by himself. So neat, so skilled,
trapping and turning, back-heeling
to some invisible team mate,
his pitch a slant of sand
between outcrops of rock
shaggy with weed and limpets,
his bare feet hopping
over an opponent stone.

The sea creeps in and will in time
call time, but in this time, this moment,
no other thing intrudes on his playing
or on the watching as someone
is struck to stillness at the sandstone wall.

Fast

The heart beats in double time,
running at quaver speed
rather than crochets,
not quavering but keeping up
a rapid trot like ponies
matching pace with thoroughbreds.
Rests are not restful,
semibreves a dream for gasping lungs
but some greater continuum
uses the fleeting seconds as it can.

The armies of perfection are most beautiful,
helmet feathers waving in the sun,
lances slanting like blown corn,
so good, so generous, so warm,
so oath-bound to serve life
even when life is off somewhere,
flirting outrageously with the dark-cloaked
seductive musician
who will play 'The Last Post'.

Outpatients

The hospital is not always this loud.
Blue scrubs are not usually
topped off with Father Christmas hats
or waiting areas plied with mince pies
baked by the Friends. Even Reception
has let its hair down, tinsel-wreathed.

Beside the automatic doors
a woman is phoning. 'They'll fit me in
as soon as they can. There is some risk…
but look, darling, to die anaesthetised
wouldn't be bad, would it? And they
think there's quite a good chance it will work.
Can't hope for more than that, can you?'

Brown plastic reindeer horns poke out
from the bag beside her swollen feet.
Children in the Christmas dawn
will fly with weightless cloven hooves
and she, the kindly moon, will watch,
even when she cannot speak to them.

Notes on Doctors

When the body starts to let you down
avoid the dry doctor who shuffles
case notes with a sigh. (Last one
before lunch, thank God.)

The lovely thing
is the consultant whose handshake
is warm, breaking through the gap between
expert and sufferer. It says
We are both people, but for one of us
luck has rusted up a bit.

Miracle

A child grown up in war gets used to fear.
Careless Talk Costs Lives.
Spies may be anywhere, danger
is intimate, almost a friend.

Bombing raids were not predictable,
unlike the morning train at eight fourteen,
timetable sacrosanct, excuses
unacceptable, exam dates fixed.

On the air-raid shelter wall
an oil lamp rocked.
Morning showed more tiles gone from the roof,
windows edged with their own broken glass,

shrapnel embedded in the lawn, the usual thing.
It all brought confidence. *I am alive.*
Good if the water main was on,
no queueing at the stand-pipe in the street.

Peace was an anti-climax.
Boredom came. Go with a man,
such a wild liar you never ask his name.
Bear a child. *To give away*, parents insist.

*You are our daughter. We will not let you
ruin your life.* They never knew
how addictive ruination is.

After half a century he phones.
I am your son.
And so we meet

in long-dreamed-of embrace.
Being unsafe
can sometimes bring a miracle.

Early Bus

Headlights breast the hill,
too far off for any sound
except the tide's wash
slapping the sea wall.

The indicator winks,
engine chuntering,
windows steamed up,
a fug of talk inside
like a travelling pub.
Up two steps, pass ready.

Harbour, love?

Yes, please.

Doors have hissed shut.
The insect bus
creeps on towards Brodick, while outside
dawn tears the black sky open
like a tangerine.

Van

The old split-screen VW van
never achieved such speed as seventy.
It had six-volt electrics that could not
do lights and heater and at the same time warn
others that we were about to turn.

I'd talk to it sometimes
on a hot Italian road
or the slow lane of a motorway
with hours to go.
I wrangled its back seat
into a bed at night when mountain rain
drummed on its roof.

And at the end
when rust like sciatica
ate up its joints, it made
a still obliging home for hens,
a nesting place where they
laid their warm eggs.

Whisper

'You must have your teeth out,'
my dead mother whispers.
'The man who will do it is here.
This morning he pulled out the teeth
of Miss Murphy at the bank
and of five men painting a white line
down the road
and of the woman who tied her dog
to the Co-op trolley rack.'

She whispers on.

'Lie down, my love.
I will pin your arms close by your sides
and then the man can pull out all your teeth
nice and easily.'

She adds, 'What did you say?'

The answer rises from a dark childhood.

'Thank you for having me.'

The weight of her is terrible.
I wish I could believe she is dead.

A Phrase of Chopin

Suddenly a heartache grips,
not just in the blackbird evening
but at midday when buses run
and the phone rings with messages
from a recorded voice.

It only takes a phrase of Chopin
or a memory of bewilderment
on some lost childhood day
and there it is again, pricking the eyes,
contracting the throat.

The stoic half-century
of loss and misplaced love
piled up a debt that must be paid
with no known money, only these
instalments of sadness.

Centenary

A hundred years ago, nineteen-fifteen,
my father crouched in a trench in Flanders.
A dead man's hand, he said,
projected from the muddy wall,
useful to lean your rifle on.
It was the only story he told
except for the one about the captain's horse
bringing him home drunk from the estaminet.
I knew him in another war,
crouched in another bolthole underground.
The hurricane lamp would flicker when
shock pulsed through the earth from a close bomb.
His hands, clamped round an empty beer glass,
trembled. We pretended not to see,
because there is nothing so dangerous
as being afraid.

Enquiry

What are you going to do? I need to know.

We will slice through your breast bone,
remove a rib and stop your heart
then connect you to a machine
that does the job equally well.
The next thing is to cut your heart open
and replace its faulty valve,
much as you would in an engine.
That being done,
the heart is kick-started
and with any luck
will run like new.

Heart

So gamble.
Cut the heart,
stake your lot
on even odds
or odd evens,
their either/or,
their or/either
or neither.
Faites vos jeux,
the red or black,
a life or burial
to play for.
Same old game.
You always knew
life is not safe.

Writers' Visits

Gone now, the school visits,
books heavy in the bag while mooching
round a tarmac yard with no way in.

The posh establishments still had
entrances, with steps sometimes,
the rest a locked door near the bins,
meant to deter gun maniacs
and wandering writers.

Reading, explaining, answering,
even discussing occasionally,
all vanished like light rain that's been absorbed
into half-gardened earth where hardy weeds
grow better than more cherished blooms.

I'm still not clear about what was achieved
except a passing streak of interest.
They e-mail now.
It's cheaper.

Grass

There has come
a great impatience with all time-wasting
and all pretence. Only what hurts
and what is beautiful can matter now,
the rest can go.
Introductions, presentations, politesse,
can blow away, less real
than the tall grass that grows
among the strawberries
and makes fine seed.

Connected

I keep a watchful eye on what is happening,
observe the breathlessness,

note the blood count, put a finger on
the gallop of the pulse,

remember what they showed me on the screen.
So beautiful, that frosted white bracken

growing deep down in the lungs, and yet
so ludicrous to think it lovely.

The brain watches, dispassionate.
Interesting. A survival rate

between three and five years.
Three years now gone.

It is quite calm.
The distance between it and condemned lungs

is like the gap between the window pane
and the moon caught in its rectangle,

shining with borrowed light
millennia away. It will remain

connected until the occurrence
of the vast unknown.

Lettuce

Do not regard me as mere stuff.
With a sharp blade, amputate
me from my root, then treat
me as you would a bunch of flowers.

Let me drink, and I will let you take
leaf upon leaf until you reach
my harmless, gentle, sensitive
young heart.

Newborn

The windscreen wiper on the left-hand side
has picked up a dead leaf.
The bread knife
is newly well-known to the hand.
Waking at five happens again
and seems for the first time. The days
are numbered now, so their component parts,
their nanoseconds, come as miracles,
shining.

Wild Horse

Child, come down
from playing in the apple tree,
it's time for you to be
bitted and bridled, broken in.
What use is a wild horse except
to its own self? Come down.
It will not hurt, except
for moments in the night,
weeping for the things that might have been.

The White Petal

Go back to the flower place.
Where is the flower place?

It is where you came from
but did not know.

This time, concentrate on
discarding the mind's protective skin.

Place a finger on the white petal
before it turns brown.

Leaves

There are times when death
seems overly insistent,
its hem-tugging tiresome.
My mother felt that way
I think. The Irish matron
who phoned told me,
'Your mother died hard, darling.
She wanted it, she'd refused food
but at the end she fought,
dear Jesus, how she fought.'

I went out from the call
into a garden by flat fields,
not the place where she waited,
a little truculent. She had held me
in her arms when I was small,
showed me the cherry leaves,
sun blasting through.
I dream of that sometimes
and know again the certainty
that she will let me fall.

Goronwy

My husband had this Luger,
a heavy, six-shot pistol.
You had to support your firing hand
with the other one, or it kicked up.
Its live bullets were kept in his desk drawer
but he fired blanks to start school sports events,
the bang so loud that kids went off
as though cordite-propelled.

When the police cracked down
on illegal firearms, he dropped it
in the Thames, and was content
(if that could ever be the word for him)
with his two shotguns and a beautiful
well-balanced hunting rifle.
There wasn't much you could say for him
except he was almost never boring.

Safe House

For true danger, an unsuitable man
must fall in love with you
and you with him. During the honeymoon,
staring from a high window down into
some street in Paris while he sleeps,
the thought will come, *What have I done?*

All that follows will be frightening.
Pregnant, you rest your hand on your belly
and think, *I will try hard to protect you.*
But you can't. You will placate, trade sex
for moments of kindness, hope your friends
still care for you, and always, always
try to understand the way he is,
though that's the last thing he will want.

Sometimes, when he is quiet, you will think
you may be safe. You will be wrong.
There is no ground between your feet,
the dream you entered will not let you go.
Each word, each glance, each gesture,
even each silence will be perilous.
After his death, uncertainty and danger
become a beautiful and very safe
new way of life.

Little Boat

The little boat of beaten gold
is a pointed dish with oars
as thin as cats' whiskers.
Sometimes the museum shifts it.

Where is the little boat
of beaten gold?
With the golden torques
and hollow golden globes.

These too are beautiful,
but the little golden boat
comes from an ancient dream
that seems like memory.

Nunc et in hora mortis nostrae

It's very old, this singing
with no conductor and no instrument,
sometimes monastic, sometimes a madrigal
for joy or lament. *Weep, O Mine Eyes*,
the rising thirds a creeping grief.

If not running well, do it again.
It's the trying hard, the coming right,
that brings us to this table with its water jug,
to listen and sing.

This book is set in Joanna, the typeface designed by the artist, stonecutter and typographer Eric Gill in the early 1930s. It was named after one of his daughters. 'A book face', Gill described it as, 'free from all fancy business.' He chose Joanna for setting his own book on page design and typesetting, *An Essay on Typography* (1931).